Romancing the Southland

The Romantic and Unusual in Southern California

by

Robert Badal

Published by
Douglas A. Campbell/
Romancing the West, Inc.

Published by
DOUGLAS A. CAMPBELL/ROMANCING THE WEST, INC.
A Dacamp Venture
P.O. Box 349
Hollywood, California 90078
(213) 874-6370

First Edition, 1994

LIBRARY OF CONGRESS CATALOGING-IN-PUBLICATION DATA
Badal, Robert, 1955-
Romancing the Southland: the romantic and unusual in Southern California/
by Robert Badal.
Edited by Michael Easterbrook and Carol Stanton.

p.   cm.
Includes Index
ISBN 0-9642332-0-7

1. Los Angeles—history, culture—guide.
2. Southern California—history, culture—guide.
3. Restaurants—guide.
4. Architecture—Southern California.
5. Travel—Southern California
I. Title.

Typesetting, book and cover designs by James P. Allen and Suzanne Matsumiya of
Graphic Touch Design & Printing, San Pedro, California
Front cover map courtesy of California Map & Travel Center, Santa Monica

Printed in the United States of America.

*The author and editors have made every effort to include accurate addresses, phone numbers and hours of
operation of each listing as of the printing of this book. We regret any errors or omissions, they are
not intentional. If you would like to update your listing please send a card to :
Romancing the West, Inc., P.O. Box 349, Hollywood, CA 90078.*